A Safe Haven

by Lara Bove

PEARSON

Scott
Foresman

Editorial Offices: Glenview, Illinois • Parsippany, New Jersey • New York, New York
Sales Offices: Needham, Massachusetts • Duluth, Georgia • Glenview, Illinois
Coppell, Texas • Ontario, California • Mesa, Arizona

ISBN: 0-328-13522-4

1 2 3 4 5 6 7 8 9 10 V0G1 14 13 12 11 10 09 08 07 06 05

People in Danger

During World War II, many people were trying to leave Europe. They were escaping from the German armies that were taking over Europe by order of the Nazi party. Adolf Hitler, the leader of the Nazis, became the ruler of Germany in 1933. He believed that Jewish people, handicapped people, Gypsies, and other groups of people were "inferior." Hitler wanted to eliminate all of these people, especially the Jews. As soon as he took power, he began making laws that took away their civil and legal rights. Then, in 1939, Hitler had his armies invade Poland, provoking England and France to declare war on Germany. World War II had begun.

The Nazis invaded and attacked most of Europe. In each country they conquered, they tried to round up and kill all the "inferior" people, in what became known as the Holocaust. To avoid becoming victims of the **Holocaust,** many people needed to escape from Europe as soon as they could.

1933 Adolf Hitler comes to power in Germany. He immediately begins taking away the civil and legal rights of Jewish people.

1939 The Nazis invade Poland; World War II begins.

1942 The American government learns about the Holocaust.

1944 The War Refugee Board is created by Congress to help European refugees.

Working for Change

Many refugees wanted to come to the United States. In 1938 more than 300,000 German refugees applied to enter the country. However, many of them were prevented from entering due to the U.S. immigration **quotas.**

These quotas allowed very few people to enter the country. Some Americans wanted to help war refugees who were on the run from the German armies. They lobbied to change the laws governing quotas. But many others did not want these refugees coming to our country. In the end the U.S. government did little to help these troubled immigrants.

Refugees came from many different countries. A visa was required to enter the United States.

The War Refugee Board

In 1944 President Franklin Roosevelt created the War Refugee Board. Its mission was to save the refugees of World War II. The War Refugee Board learned about the Nazi concentration camps through the eyewitness accounts of surivors who had escaped them. **Concentration camps** were places the Nazis set up to imprison and exterminate people. The Board used the survivors' accounts to alert the world to the crimes that the Nazis were committing.

Along with trying to draw attention to what was going on in the concentration camps, the War Refugee Board also worked to turn an old army base in Oswego, New York, into a refugee shelter. When the shelter was ready, President Roosevelt sent an official to Italy to bring a group of refugees to the United States to live at it.

About three thousand people applied to be brought to the shelter, even though Roosevelt had only given permission for one thousand. The refugees came from all over Europe. Among them were people who were Jewish, Catholic, Greek Orthodox, and Protestant. There were individuals of all ages, from the elderly to small babies.

The Trip Across the Atlantic

In all, 982 refugees were taken to a ship called the *Henry Gibbins*. Once aboard, they were introduced to Ruth Gruber, an official from the United States government. Gruber spoke German, the primary language of most of the refugees, so she became the refugees' representative and **translator.** When a refugee needed to talk with someone who did not speak German, such as an American official, Ruth would translate for them.

Translating was only a small part of Ruth Gruber's job. She also listened to each person's story. The stories Gruber heard were horrific. They involved refugees' family members being killed, their homes being destroyed, and the refugees themselves being imprisoned in concentration camps. Gruber carefully wrote down their stories so that she would later be able to tell the world what had happened. The refugees were grateful to Ruth. They trusted her and went to her for whatever they needed.

Ruth Gruber (circled) was aboard the ship to help the refugees as they journeyed to the United States.

Life on the *Henry Gibbins*

The *Henry Gibbins* was an Army transport ship, built to carry soldiers and equipment. This made it uncomfortable for the refugees. Among other things, they were forced to sleep in bunks stacked three high.

Crowded living conditions made the trip difficult.

The refugees were not the only ones aboard the *Henry Gibbins.* The ship also carried soldiers who were injured or had finished their **tours of duty.** At first the soldiers were separated from the refugees, but as the days wore on, the rules were relaxed. Among the refugees were opera singers and other kinds of performers. They danced and sang for the soldiers. The soldiers gave the children treats such as chewing gum and coins. Some refugees passed the time by taking English classes each afternoon.

The refugees were fed two meals a day, which may not seem like enough. But since they had been starved by the Nazis, it was the most they had eaten in a long time. Some of the foods were quite familiar to the refugees. Other foods were new. For instance, one of the refugees confused white bread with cake!

After having starved in Europe (below left), the refugees ate much better aboard the ship.

America, at Last

On August 3, 1944, the *Henry Gibbins* arrived in New York harbor. The trip across the Atlantic had taken thirteen days. That day, the soldiers left the ship. The refugees spent one more night on board.

The next day, the refugees took a train to the Oswego refugee shelter, now called the Fort Ontario Emergency Refugee Shelter. Many of these passengers had been taken by force to concentration camps on trains. Others had seen their family members taken away on trains. This train ride was much different. The people sat in passenger cars, and they were being taken to a place where they would be kept safe.

The Jewish refugees ate their meals together at the shelter in Oswego.

Arriving at the Shelter

Some of the refugees experienced a shock upon seeing the shelter for the first time. The shelter's barbed wire reminded them too much of the concentration camps from which they had escaped. But in Oswego the barbed wire was meant as a safety measure, to help ensure that everyone stayed healthy. The U.S. government was worried that the refugees might have diseases. So they were put under **quarantine** for one month. Quarantine meant that until the refugees were proven to be healthy, they couldn't have contact with people outside the shelter.

Despite the quarantine the refugees were treated well. Most importantly, they were given plenty of food. They were served hot coffee, cold milk, cornflakes, white bread, peanut butter, and hard-boiled eggs. Families were housed together. For the first time in years, everyone got to sleep in clean, comfortable beds.

U.S. **customs agents** checked the people's belongings. They were shocked when they saw suitcases holding nothing but a few family photos or some torn clothing.

Americans Help the Refugees

During the quarantine, the refugees weren't allowed to leave the shelter. However, the residents of Oswego often spoke to them through the shelter's fence. They did their best to make the refugees feel welcome.

One woman thought the refugees might like a bicycle to ride, so she passed hers over the fence. She also determined to speak to them face-to-face. So she went home and dressed as a refugee. The disguise worked! She was able to sneak under the fence and talk directly with the refugees.

The shelter, having been a military base, had showers that were difficult for the refugees to get used to. Designed for men only, they were large and open. There weren't any curtains to separate one bather from the next. So Ruth Gruber asked the Rochester, New York, chapter of the National Council on Jewish Women to help sew shower curtains. The chapter gladly sewed the shower curtains. They also sewed window curtains, bedspreads, and more!

One of the shelter's most touching stories involved a customs agent. The agent went to a local store on his lunch hour and bought a pair of pants, a shirt, and a jacket. When he returned to the shelter, he gave the clothing to a man who owned only one shirt.

Another wonderful story involved a girl named Susan Saunders. Susan was a nine-year-old girl from Oswego. She passed her own doll through the fence to one of the refugees, who was about her age.

Some refugees, like the man who owned only one shirt, had left their homes with only the clothes they wore. Compared to some, they were lucky. Those who had been prisoners had only the clothes they had been forced to wear in the concentration camps. Most of the refugees had no shoes. The people of Oswego responded to the refugees' needs with great compassion. Many of them went home and gathered clothing, children's shoes, cookies, and candies. Then they passed them through or over the fence.

Refugee children being looked after by U.S. military police.

13

The First Weeks at Oswego

From the very beginning the refugees tried to live normal lives, despite the hardships imposed by the quarantine. One couple was married during that first month. Others were married later.

The refugees also began to think about issues of daily life. They wanted to know what to do about educating their children. Should teachers come to the refugee shelter, or should the children go to the schools in Oswego? They wanted to do something about the white bread as well. Most of the refugees were from Eastern Europe, where they were used to heavy bread made from dark-colored grain. They couldn't get used to the taste of the American bread.

The refugees turned to Ruth Gruber for help. She had a bakery put in the camp so the refugees could bake their own bread. She also addressed the issue of how the refugee children would be educated. Gruber helped convince the government that once the quarantine ended it would be OK for refugee childeren to attend the Oswego public schools.

Refugee teenagers attended Oswego High School.

Other Daily Life Issues

Most of the refugees were Jewish. They needed to eat food that was **kosher,** or made according to Jewish religious rules. Jewish people who follow the kosher rules cannot eat pork. Nor can they eat meat and dairy foods at the same meal. Kosher food has to be prepared and eaten on special dishes. People must make sure that the dishes have never been used for foods that are not kosher and that the same dishes are never used for both meat and dairy foods. This was a problem, because the dishes at the shelter did not meet this rule.

Again, the people asked Ruth Gruber to help them. She spoke with two leaders from Agudath Israel, a Jewish group that understood all the kosher rules. Within a day Agudath Israel had new dishes delivered for the refugee shelter's kosher kitchen.

Kosher food-preparation rules require that separate dishes be used for meat and dairy products.

15

Fall 1944

The quarantine ended on September 1, 1944, a month after the refugees disembarked from the *Henry Gibbins*. To celebrate, the Fort Ontario Emergency Refugee Shelter held an open house. The open house allowed outsiders to see how the refugees lived. Residents of Oswego, the refugees' friends and relatives, and reporters and photographers all came and took pictures of the shelter and the refugees.

That fall the Oswego schools admitted almost two hundred refugees as students. School was hard for the children because they did not speak English well. Still, they had a great desire to learn. They wanted to make up for the years of schooling they had lost while living on the run or in concentration camps in Europe.

The following spring several young adults went to college. The rest of the adults were able to take classes at the shelter. Five hundred adult students were allowed to enroll in twenty-nine different classes. They learned English, carpentry, painting, sculpture, sewing, and more.

In late 1944 young refugees began attending school in Oswego.

Concerns About the Future

The refugees worried about what would happen after the war. They had promised to return to their home countries. As the war went on, however, it became clear that there was little reason for them to return to Europe. Their countries were no longer the same. Many of the people whom they had known and loved were dead. Governments had changed, and cities had been destroyed.

The refugees' futures seemed hopeless. Even worse, the U.S. government refused to reverse its decision. President Roosevelt still planned to send the refugees back to Europe after the war ended. Ruth Gruber was working hard to try and prevent this from happening.

In April of 1945, World War II was close to its end. It was reported in the newspapers that the Fort Ontario Emergency Refugee Shelter would close on June 30. Ruth Gruber denied the news, but it had been printed in the newspapers. Whom were the refugees to believe?

Scenes of destruction such as these made the refugees unhappy at the idea of having to return to Europe.

The War Ends

The war in Europe ended with Germany's surrender on May 7, 1945. But the refugees at Oswego still didn't know their fate. How long would they live at the shelter? Would they have to return to Europe? Even though the Nazis were defeated, returning to Europe might not mean freedom, as harsh governments controlled by the Soviet Union were being set up in many European countries. This was another reason why the refugees hoped that the U.S. government would allow them to live here.

On July 4, 1945, the U.S. government changed the rules slightly. Now the refugees could travel twenty miles from the shelter. They could also have overnight visitors at the camp. It was a welcome change, but it was not true freedom.

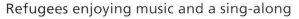

Refugees enjoying music and a sing-along

Freedom at Last

On December 22, 1945, President Harry Truman announced that any Oswego refugee could apply for a visa, a paper that gives a person permission to enter a country. This was almost six months after the war had ended.

One week later, on New Year's Eve, the people had a celebration at the Oswego shelter. They were sure that they would be allowed to go free in the coming year.

Once again, many Americans wanted to help the refugees. Seventy different communities, from large cities to small towns, offered to help them resettle. People from California to New York all wanted to help the refugees find housing, jobs, and schools.

Freed Jewish refugees marched beneath a banner that read "Long Live the Great President of the U.S., Truman, and the American People!"

U. S. law said that the refugees had to leave the country and then reenter before they could live here legally. On January 17, 1946, they rode buses to Ontario, Canada. They went over the Rainbow Bridge and into the town of Niagara Falls, where they met with an American official. He gave each refugee a United States visa. Now they could enter the country and travel wherever they wished!

Some of the refugees went right back to New York, to the office of the National Refugee Service. Here they reunited with family members. Over the next few days, the refugees resettled in different parts of the country and began making the most of their new lives. They moved to about seventy different communities. Many got jobs, while others decided to go to college. Some went on to make great contributions to the world as doctors, professors, and business leaders. The refugees never forgot the chance they had been given to live in safety and freedom.

In 1946, refugee children finally got the chance to live freely in the United States.

Now Try This

Be a Historian

The book you have just read provides much information about the Oswego shelter. However, you can supplement that information by doing your own historical research. Follow the steps on page 23 in order to learn more.

1. Think about the book you just read. What people or topics would you like to learn more about? Make a chart like the one shown below. In the Topic column, write down as many topics as you can. You should think of at least four topics. Your topics can include people.
2. Now, think about each topic in the first column. What are some questions you have about that topic or person? You might ask, "What did Ruth Gruber do after the refugees left?" Try to think of at least three questions for each topic, and write them in the Questions column.

Topic	Questions	Where to Find Answers	Answers

3. Next, think about what kind of sources might provide answers to your questions. Write down those sources in the Where to Find Answers column.
4. Finally, in the Answers column, write down the answers to at least three of your questions, using the sources you listed in the Where to Find Answers column. Were you surprised by what you learned?

Glossary

concentration camps *n.* camps used by the Nazis to imprison and kill people they thought were inferior, especially Jewish people.

customs agents *n.* people who inspect materials that travelers bring into countries.

Holocaust *n.* the term given to the Nazis' systematic killing of six million Jews during World War II.

kosher *adj.* made according to Jewish religious rules for preparing food.

quarantine *n.* a rule that keeps people from having contact with other people for a period of time.

quotas *n.* numbers that tell how many people can emigrate from different countries.

tours of duty *n.* the amounts of time soldiers serve their countries.

translator *n.* someone who helps people communicate with each other. The translator is able to speak more than one language.